WILDLIFE OF CANADA
EXPLORING CANADA
Lynn Stone

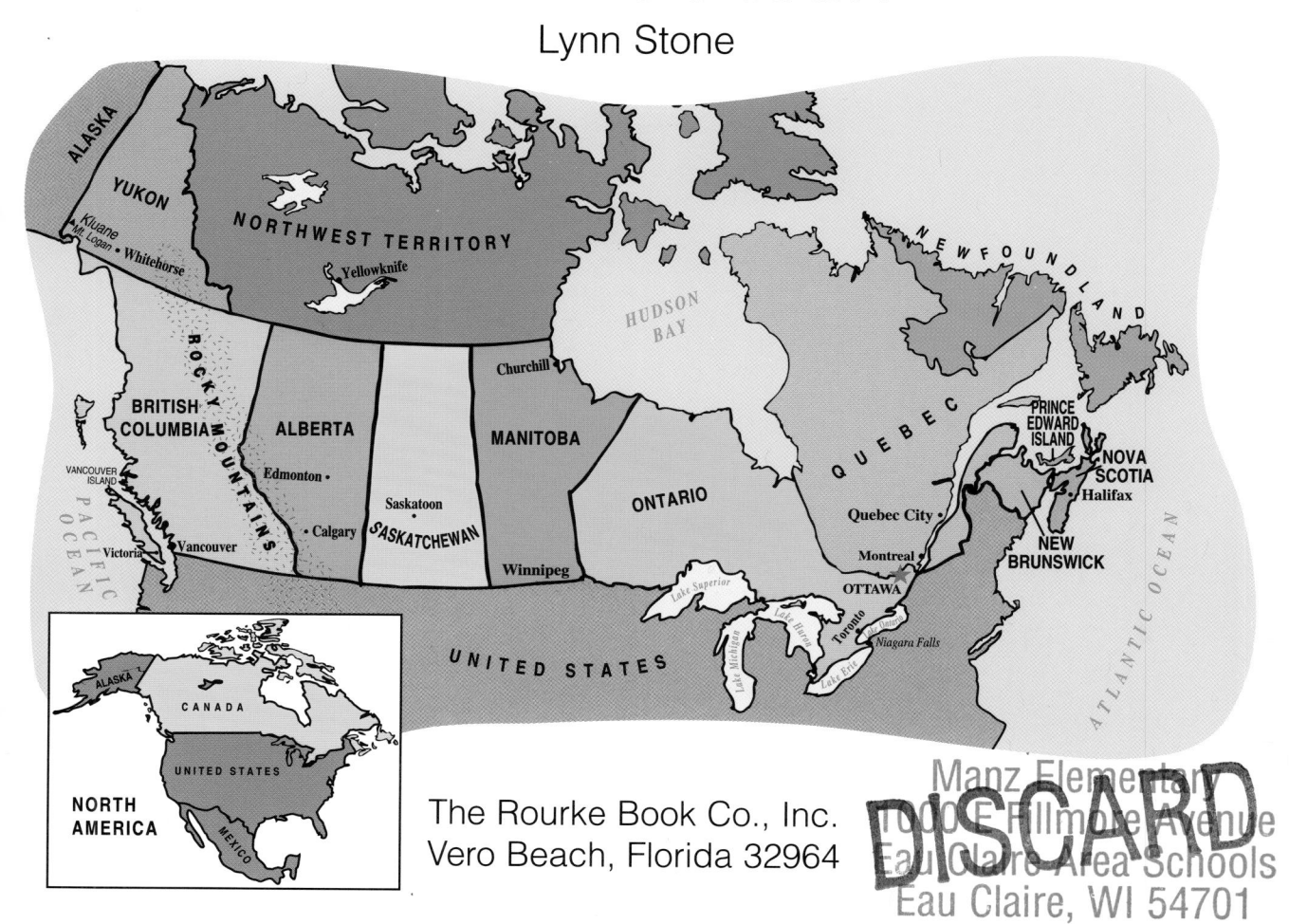

The Rourke Book Co., Inc.
Vero Beach, Florida 32964

Edited by Sandra A. Robinson and
Pamela J.P. Schroeder

PHOTO CREDITS
All photos © Lynn M. Stone except pages 8 and 15 © Tom and
Pat Leeson

Library of Congress Cataloging-in-Publication Data

Stone, Lynn M.
    Wildlife of Canada / by Lynn Stone.
    p. cm. — (Exploring Canada)
    Includes index.
    ISBN 1-55916-104-3
    1. Zoology—Canada—Juvenile literature. [1. Zoology—
Canada. 2. Animals.] I. Title. II. Series.
QL219.S86   1995
591.971—dc20   94-47361
                                                CIP
                                                AC

Printed in the USA

TABLE OF CONTENTS

WILDLIFE OF CANADA

Canada's rivers, lakes, forests, marshes, oceans, seashores, mountains, prairies and **tundra** are homes for great numbers of wild animals.

Canada is a huge country—only Russia is larger. Canada is an excellent home for wildlife because so few people live there. More than 425 **species,** or kinds, of birds and 93 species of mammals live in Canada.

Some of Canada's biggest land animals are polar bears, grizzly bears, wolves, moose and **caribou.**

Caribou live in northern Canada and Newfoundland

SEA ANIMALS

Canada's largest animals live in the oceans along its shores. The biggest is the blue whale. It can be 85 feet (26 meters) long and weigh more than 230,000 pounds (104,545 kilograms).

White whales (belugas), killer whales (orcas) and thousands of seals and sea lions live in Canadian seas.

Many sea birds, such as puffins, eat Canada's ocean fish.

A group of killer whales (orcas) cruises along the coast of Vancouver Island, British Columbia

SEASHORE ANIMALS

Puffins and other sea birds nest on cliffs along Canada's seashores. Below rocky cliffs, sea urchins, starfish and sea anemones live in tide pools. Shore birds race along the surf and hunt in the wet nooks between rocks.

In northern Canada, polar bears prowl along the coasts and the ice that forms each winter on Arctic seas. The polar bears eat seals.

A polar bear prowls the sea ice of Hudson Bay

ANIMALS OF RIVERS AND LAKES

River otters, mink and brown bears hunt in and along Canada's waterways. The brown bears look for the great **schools** of Pacific salmon that travel up the rivers each summer and fall.

Six species of Pacific salmon live in the rivers of western Canada. Another species, the Atlantic salmon, lays its eggs in a few rivers of eastern Canada.

Canada's lakes are homes for trout and pike— and for the fish hawks that catch them.

Sockeye salmon travel from the ocean into clear, fast rivers in western Canada each summer and fall

Brightly colored Atlantic puffins live on shore cliffs in northeastern Canada

A snow goose sits on its nest on Canada's Arctic tundra

TUNDRA ANIMALS

Much of northern Canada is windy and treeless. A carpet of tiny, low-lying plants covers the ground. This is the tundra, a summer home for millions of birds—ducks, geese, tundra swans, sandpipers, gulls and others.

Small herds of musk ox graze on the tundra. Hundreds of thousands of caribou graze there, too.

Wolves living on the tundra hunt the caribou herds. Arctic foxes, snowy owls and weasels eat the tundra ground squirrels, hares and lemmings.

Musk oxen gather on the tundra of the Northwest Territories in fall

MOUNTAIN ANIMALS

The high country of Canada's cold, jagged mountain peaks is home to bighorn sheep, elk, mule deer, mountain lions, grizzly bears, **pikas,** mountain goats and many other animals.

Each fall most of the mountain animals travel south into the shelter of forests and valleys. Marmots and ground squirrels hide in their burrows, or underground homes, and sleep winter away.

The mountain goats face winter in the mountains. They use their hooves to clear snow from plants they eat.

Bighorn sheep live in the high country of Canada's Rocky Mountains

FOREST ANIMALS

Thick forest covers much of southern and central Canada. Most of the forest trees are needle-leaved evergreens—"Christmas trees."

The Canadian forests are homes for hunters like wolverines, wolves, martens, fishers and Canada lynxes. They eat squirrels, rabbits, rodents and birds. Grouse and many smaller birds nest in the evergreen forests.

Moose like forest ponds and marshes, where they feed on **aquatic** plants.

The howls of wolves echo in Canada's forests

PRAIRIE ANIMALS

Prairies are lands covered by wild grasses and other plants. Few trees grow in the prairies. The roots of prairie grasses are so thick that trees cannot find a place to plant their roots!

Canada's prairies are in the southern parts of the **provinces** of Alberta, Saskatchewan and Manitoba. Pronghorns, mule deer, plains buffalo, prairie dogs, coyotes and several species of birds share the prairies.

Millions of ducks nest on Canada's prairie ponds and marshes, which are sometimes called "duck factories."

American bison (buffalo) still live in some of Canada's prairie parks

ANIMALS OF THE NATIONAL PARKS

Canada has more than 35 national parks. Each one is a home for wild animals.

Wood Buffalo National Park protects thousands of wood buffalo and the extremely rare whooping crane.

Jasper National Park has herds of elk, deer and bighorn sheep. Wolves live there, too.

The forests of Newfoundland's Terra Nova National Park protect black bears, Canada lynxes and woodland caribou.

Glossary

aquatic (uh KWAT ihk) — of or related to water, such as an *aquatic* bird

caribou (KARE uh boo) — a large, northern cousin of deer; wild reindeer

pika (PI kuh) — a very small, plump mammal that lives in North America's western mountains

province (PRAH vints) — any one of the 10 statelike regions, which together with two territories, make up Canada

school (SKOOL) — a group of fish traveling together

species (SPEE sheez) — within a group of closely-related animals, one certain kind, such as an *Arctic* fox

tundra (TUN druh) — the treeless carpet of low-lying plants in the Far North and on mountains above the tree line

INDEX